Texting Guide

How to Use the Perfect Words and
Secret Texting Strategies

*(How to Influence, Persuade and Seduce Anyone
via Text Message)*

Ray Mock

Published By **Darby Connor**

Ray Mock

All Rights Reserved

Texting Guide: How to Use the Perfect Words and Secret Texting Strategies (How to Influence, Persuade and Seduce Anyone via Text Message)

ISBN 978-1-77485-918-6

No part of this guidebook shall be reproduced in any form without permission in writing from the publisher except in the case of brief quotations embodied in critical articles or reviews.

Legal & Disclaimer

The information contained in this ebook is not designed to replace or take the place of any form of medicine or professional medical advice. The information in this ebook has been provided for educational & entertainment purposes only.

The information contained in this book has been compiled from sources deemed reliable, and it is accurate to the best of the Author's knowledge; however, the Author cannot guarantee its accuracy and validity and cannot be held liable for any errors or omissions. Changes are periodically made to this book. You must consult your doctor or get professional medical advice before using any of the suggested remedies, techniques, or information in this book.

Upon using the information contained in this book, you agree to hold harmless the Author from and against any damages, costs, and expenses, including any legal fees potentially resulting from the application of any of the information provided by this guide. This disclaimer applies to any damages or injury caused by the use and application, whether directly or indirectly, of any advice or information presented, whether for breach of contract, tort, negligence, personal injury, criminal intent, or under any other cause of action.

You agree to accept all risks of using the information presented inside this book. You need to consult a professional medical practitioner in order to ensure you are both able and healthy enough to participate in this program.

Table of contents

Chapter 1: How to get her a phone number.. 1

Chapter 2: Sexting like A Pro 10

Chapter 3: Keep her entertained by your texts 17

Chapter 4: What To Read? 27

Chapter 5: What makes great texting possible?... 32

Chapter 6: Texting Strategies 38

Chapter 7: Common Mistakes While Texting 46

Chapter 8: Mindset To Text Success............ 61

Chapter 9: How to send a first text message to a girl. 65

Chapter 10: Get his attention with a text 74

Chapter 11: Attracting with Texts 88

Chapter 12: Captain her ship of emotions... 92

Chapter 13: Getting the Love Machine in Gear With Sexting 101

Chapter 14: Keep her interested in your texts 105

Chapter 15: How to Keep Multiple Women Happy at the Same Time 108

Chapter 16: Flirtexting Vs Sexting 120

Chapter 17: How to Respect It With Class and Sass 127

Chapter 18: Influencing Someone Through Text 143

Chapter 19: Tips for keeping things spicy with sexting 157

Chapter 20: How You Build and Maintain Attraction 163

Chapter 21: What Not to Text 168

Chapter 22: Building Comfort 177

Conclusion 184

Chapter 1: How to get her a phone number

It's a scary first step in any relationship, and we all know it. Many of us have failed to make the first steps in our quest to get to know someone. The book will teach you how to do this without feeling nervous or scared. It is important to remember that people who fail to get a lady's number do so because they are doing it in the wrong manner. There is no right or wrong way. You will look foolish and be rejected.

Let us start by looking at it in the wrong direction. We can then correct them and help you become a winner when you reach for the target's number.

The Wrong Way To Ask for Her Number - It is not appropriate to sound as though you are borrowing her permission to have her number. Most men will ask for her number in the same way that they do every day: "Can you give me your number?" This makes you appear much lower than the woman to whom you want to be intimate. You must show value by your approach. This is how you can ask for the number. Don't make it seem like you need the number urgently, but do ask for it in a way you truly want to communicate with her.

It is not easy but it is possible. It is important to remember that you are not inferior to the lady in this situation. Asking for permission to call the number will make it sound like you don't trust the lady. By asking for the phone number so low, you will be displaying insecurity. Insecurity is a big turnoff for women. Do you want to turn off a beautiful woman before you reveal your feelings to it? You have to be bold enough about it.

It is important that your request does not ask for a yes or no answer. This is because if you form your request in the same way as the question above, the target will be unable to choose whether or not to answer you. This could lead to rejections of up to 50%.

Some men believe that by giving their number first to the woman they need, it will attract her attention. Offering your number first to the lady if you don't have her number is not a good idea. The message you are trying tell her is that she should search for you by calling later after the meeting. This is a NO for ladies. After you have received the number from the woman, you can offer to exchange yours.

Feminism was a part of human history since before time began. It is still a popular belief. When a woman is ready to meet a man, it's not normal for her to ask for his number. While it is unacceptable socially for women to pursue men, there are exceptions. But you shouldn't expect women to call you back immediately after the first meeting.

number.

A beauty who appears obsessed with men is viewed as a woman who is desperate to attract men. One does not want to be seen as a slut, or to have their face ruined by trying to get a man. You will be willing to wait until you get called.

The women will not be willing to give up the fantasy of being hunted, so taking the number and acting upon it will prevent her from experiencing that romantic feeling when you are trying to lure them into your nest. They love to be seduced.

This is not the right way to ask for the number of a beauty product you desire. Next, we will show you how.

The Right Way to Ask for the Number. Having understood how you shouldn't ask for a girl's number, you now know that you should never ask her permission to get it. It should not be answered with a "yes or no" answer. If both the most popular ways of asking for the number aren't the best, how do you then request it?

It is possible to get out of this situation by being totally dominant and directly asking for the number. By asking the woman directly for her number (e.g. "I would like to have your number"), you can make sure that the lady isn't hesitant to accept the offer.

The dominance of men elicits attraction in women. When you do it well, she will notice how determined and focused you are to achieve what you want. Even in ancient times, men who were most dominant had the opportunity to acquire all the resources needed to provide shelter, food, clothing and shelter. Women naturally prefer strong, reliable, dominating males because they are wired to be sexually dominant.

We can't deny that stalkers are just as bad for women as they are for men. However, we don't do any less stalking than them. Let a lady know that you won't stalk her if she gives you the number. Begin by asking the lady if she has been stalked in the past and how that went. Then, air your disapproval and state how you would never do it to another person.

You should be thoughtful when asking for the number. Wrap your request with a statement that touches upon your conversation. Perhaps you pretend that your time has ended after chatting with the beautiful woman you feel a strong connection to. You could then ask for her number to keep the conversation going on text. To make sure she knows you're not a stalker, joke with her by asking her to promise her not to stalk her by sending her a slew of messages in one day. I insist that she should not be concerned about the stalking by making it seem serious. If you do, she might be misunderstood and assume that you are desperate for you.

The boldness of asking for the number does not mean that you will get it. While you may be attracted towards her, making her love you is not an easy task. Answers to these questions will include "I don't give out my number to anyone I don't know" and "It's not normal for my number to be given this fast." Make her feel attracted to your company by telling her you are open to having further conversations but you don't have the time. Let her know that you are serious and want to get to understand her.

However, the bad news is that she may object to your pleas. What do you do when she resists your pleas? Calm down. That should be your first response. Let her know that you won't call her more than once per day. If you become bored with one another, you can put an end to the calling. You can also tell her that the calling will stop. But insist that the evening is not a time for any kind of communication between you.

The goal is to make the lady feel less at-risk by giving you her phone number. If you fail to achieve this, don't worry about it. After a mature and direct conversation, you can get the number. We can then move to the next level of techniques for texting the lady you have lured into your nest.

Chapter 2: Sexting like A Pro

We discussed how to win over a guy via SMS in the previous chapter. This chapter focuses on how to send him sexy texts to get his interest and intrigue. The act is commonly known as "sexting", but it's meant to only be subtle ways of showing your interest in him. This chapter will not cover phone sex.

Put the traps in place

When you are sexting with your man (or a man you're interested in), you must make sure he knows what you mean. It is important to lay the traps in a subtle and not obvious manner. Do not place traps you are certain he'll fall into. These traps don't have to be obvious. Make him feel your thoughts and feelings.

Speak something like: "hey sexy. He wants ..." Continue that sentence in a witty way. It is important to stay true to the subject. You can continue the sentence in the next message by saying "...smooch.

Lingerie Talk

The next step is to tell him all about your lingerie. Imagine him imagining the color of your pants and how it is laced. Your brassiere is also important. Talk to him about how it supports you soft breasts. Keep it subtle and encourage him to engage in sex.

You could also tell him about the clothes you wear on the outside. Then, slowly, make him ask for the inside. Do not tell him that your clothes aren't on, as this will lead to phone sex quickly. Instead, tell your lingerie story to him and get him sexy.

Discuss Fantasies

Next, share your fantasies. You can tell him about yours, and he can ask you to tell yours. Make an effort to get to know him better and let him know that you share similar fantasies. Look for a common idea and capitalize on it. You can say to him, "I dream about tying you to your bed," and then reply, "Tying me up to my bed and having a blackfold over my eyes."

Play with him and make sure that you are always on the right page. Encourage him to be more open and honest. Don't keep repeating "yeah me also" or your similarities. You will appear to be losing interest in his ideas and simply nodding your head to his messages.

Make it Real

Many times it is simple to read someone's SMS and assess their emotions. It is important to say things like "I want you to feel my soft pantsy" and not just say it. If you don't, it will seem as though you're just trying to bag him by using sex.

He will lose interest in what you are saying and not respond to it in the right way. Keep it real and say what you mean. Don't tell him if you don't feel the same way.

Timing

It is important to choose the right time for your sexts. It is essential to know when to send them, and whether he will respond. This is why it's important to not rush and make sure you have had a chance to meet him at least twice or three times, as well as chatting with him for at minimum 2 to 3 week.

Also make sure to check his mood to see if he is feeling happy. He should also be aware that you are not sending him sexts in gloomy situations.

Be confident

If you are going to sext someone, you need to be confident. You need to be confident about yourself and your assets. You must be confident about sexting him and not be afraid being naughty. Show him that you can be a real tigress and make her want you. Confidence is a key turner and something that will make him want twice as many of you.

Pictures

Next, send pictures. You can send pictures of your lingerie if he becomes flirtatious and naughty. Make sure they look elegant and tasteful. Send him photos of you in awkward positions just to accent a specific part of the body.

He will start to lose interest if you try too hard. Make a great picture by sitting on a bed and showing off your entire body. Many men enjoy women's legs more than their boobs. You shouldn't be too focused on the sexy parts, but rather focus on his preferences.

Audio

Record a few sexy messages for him along with your texts. You can even record something sexual like "hey sexyboy, how would you like to taste something sweet?" It can be said in a sassy voice. Stress the "sexy boys" and "sweet".

You can also record your face with the video feature. Add some sexy expressions and your face will be recorded. It's important to be subtle and not seem desperate. Be a playboy bunny, and use your index fingers to call him toward you in the video recording.

Personalized Words

Men love personalized words. Give your man a nick name that is unique and creative. Avoid using the common and generic names, such as adding "boy", to your name. Instead, add a cute ending. As men of all ages prefer to be spoken in this way, you can modify your language to communicate with him.

Chapter 3: Keep her entertained by your texts

You are glad that things are going well. You know that she likes and appreciates everything you have done. Although you have learned how to text girls, it is now a difficult task. You may only text one another, which can be an integral part of any relationship. Maybe you do see each other from time to time. Whatever the case, you want to keep things interesting. Also, you want things to be spontaneous. It's not what a girl wants to get a text saying "Wassup?" They will probably not bother responding. A text saying "How're you?" is not what a girl wants.

However, all girls desire to receive messages that make them feel good and liked. They also want texts that are a little bit strange and kind. Flirtatious, if that is' where you are going!

It's time to spice things up. It's okay to send an early morning text to your girl but not every morning. Sending morning texts to your girl should be fun, original, caring, and even sexy.

Below are some lovely morning texts

"Well, I couldn't help it, woke up thinking about you this morning."

"Have a wonderful day, will think about you while going through my mathematics!"

"I understand you have a busy schedule, good luck with your meetings, you are brilliant!"

"Hope your wearing that red dress you love! Even if your not, I will imagine that you are ...'

Depending on your relationship, the red-dress text might or may not work. It's best to wait until things are really hot before you make it too saucy. You must do what works for both you and her. While you can take the ideas from this article as a guide, don't necessarily follow them. It's a nice thing to send goodnight messages!

"Sweet dreams Lucy," works just fine. It doesn't have to be much more. It shows her you care about her and encourages her to think of you even while she's sleeping. Then she will remember you when she gets up the next morning.

These are wonderful spontaneous texts. Sending early morning messages (but not every day, don't forget to keep the options open), will result in longer texts later in the day. If you worry too much about what you are going say, then you won't have much to say. Writing is all about spontaneity. Keep in mind that you are not writing texts for the Nobel Literary Prize. You are simply writing text to have fun and flirt together. Keep them honest, keep it simple and be original.

Your messages will be more than flirty. Sometimes girls can get very intense. This is not a good idea. When you are comfortable with each other, you may be able to include the following in your conversations.

Family.

Friendships.

Relationships: Past or present

Politics.

Expectations.

You may have spoken to her about her family. You asked her if there were siblings. She told you about her stepfather, brother, sister and mother. You have shared with her your family. You may not have gone into detail. Be available to listen if it feels right. If she is experiencing difficulties with her mother or other family members, listen to her. As this can make her defensive, don't ask direct questions about her mother's relationship or why she has a bad relationship with her mother. Instead, say, "I sense that you and my mom are having difficulty." If you ever need to talk, I'm available for you." You will find her eager to share the information with you.

It is possible that you are friends. When she talks about her friendships, listen carefully. She won't ever say anything negative. She may have a bad day with her best friend but they are likely to be friends the next day. You can listen to her and give gentle advice.

However, the most important thing is to make her feel you are truly listening to all she says. You can also tell her about friends, and how you wish to meet them. Because, you do!

You need to be careful about past relationships. You should not share every detail of your relationship with someone you just left. You should be honest and not share any secrets. Do not ask her about her relationships in the past. She'll be able to tell you when she is ready. It's not a good idea to text about certain things, but rather to talk about them. Wait until the right moment.

Politics. Be careful! Do your research before you decide to follow her lead. Take care if you have opposing views. It is okay to have differing opinions.

However, it is not a good idea to be too opinionated. Sometimes, it is okay to not talk about politics at all.

Expectations are an important aspect of texting. Make sure you do it when it's convenient. If you love her so much that you feel you can't tell anyone, do it. But don't frighten her away. Each relationship is unique. You might be able to communicate your expectations quickly if you both feel the same. However, keep it light at the beginning!

Even if texting goes well, it is important to learn how to make a girl love you via text. Avoid rushing to respond via text in the initial days and weeks. Make it light and fun, flirtatious and flirtatious. Only once you are both comfortable with each other's feelings, can you start to get serious about expectations and relationships.

Be sure to keep her busy, even before you begin lengthy conversations. These are all great messages to send.

"Hi Diane. Here's a picture of me and my dog at the park. We had so much fun!"

"Steve and I went hiking together today. Here we sit, amongst daisies. Miss you."

"I am in Sausalito today. See this incredible blue sea!" !"

It is not a good idea to send her photos of yourself. However, if you are doing something unusual or special, send them photographs. Send her photos of your morning scrambled eggs, but keep it exciting. Your lifestyle should keep her interested and make it possible for her to become a part. It is important to tell her you want her to be with and/or join you.

Never send pictures of you and your friends in nightclubs, drinking, or with your shirts off. These will put her off. You don't want your daughter to have FOMO.

You want her life to be real. Send her pictures of you abseiling but don't do it if you don't abseil. Keep it real!

Be there for her in times of crisis.

"Hey. Hope you're not feeling anxious about your job interview. It will be great.

"Let us know if you hear back from your sister. We hope you can sort things out."

"Remember, I'm here for you if needed."

As simple as this text may be, it is vital. Make sure she knows that you are there for her in all situations.

Keep in mind that you shouldn't be focusing on the cute, pretty, or sexy sides of girls. They want you to tell them that they are intelligent, funny, thoughtful and smart. You should tell them that these qualities are what you like about them. Also, be intelligent, funny, and thoughtful. Girls like these kinds of boys. Nowadays, girls take their liking for their personalities more than their short skirts. You need to be aware of feminism. Fight like crazy but only when it's right for you.

Chapter 4: What To Read?

Texting is a great way to impress someone. You don't need to look fancy, do so much, or act in a certain way. Simply choose the appropriate words and phrases to create the sweet messages you wish to send.

The message should be brief, but not too long. It should also leave the reader with a feeling that is still a mystery. It's a great way to keep a girl interested in the conversation and engaged.

Funny jokes and phrases can be a great way to start conversations, as was stated in the previous chapter. It's better to be creative and make your own jokes. A good sense of humor is a must for most women.

It is also helpful to use descriptive words when sending text messages. Descriptive words can be very helpful for girls because they can create a mental picture from what you are writing. It is because of this that romantic novels and stories that include many descriptive words are very popular with women. They find it fascinating to imagine the scenes through the descriptive words that an author uses. You can use it to tease your girl and to stimulate her imagination and emotions. However, you should be careful not overdo it. Texts that are too long may become boring and make the girl lose interest. You could text "My bed's so soft but my room is too cold," ..." to let her know you mean it. This will send the message that she is interested in you, but not too obvious.

You should be aware of the power and versatility of exclamation points or periods. You can add drama and intrigue to plain text messages by using them. An exclamation point or extra period can make a particular word or phrase more intense or clearer.

She can giggle by texting her pickup line lines. You can either come up with your own ideas or use others'. It is more entertaining for her if it is silly.

A cute expression of affection can make a sweet gesture. You can be sure she will remember you everytime she hears the name. It could also signal to her that she is unique.

It is best to start off with vague topics when it comes to messaging about certain topics. Avoid personal topics. Talking about her dreams and favorites can make for great text topics. You can ask your friend what her favorite food would be and add some great comments.

You can also tease the mind by asking her "Where and how do you see yourself in 10 years?"

It's a good idea to compliment her once in a while. This will show her that you care about her looks and admire her style. Every girl enjoys receiving compliments, even from her boyfriend.

Only use emoticons in text messages. It can give a text an extra edge by displaying more of what you feel. A smiley face, or wink face, can convey positive emotions.

When you create a text, it is important to take time to consider what you want to say before you send it. You can get too caught up in your emotions and end up saying too much. Texting is not an athletic sport so take your time before you send the next message.

Allow her to reply before you send another email. You might find that the time between texts is not always as long due to other factors. You may also choose to stop the conversation at certain times, in order not to appear too attached.

Chapter 5: What makes great texting possible?

You must understand the basics of texting to be able to appreciate great texting. It is about being able to communicate feelings, have stimulating conversations, and really understand what others want, need, and desire. This is the key to a healthy, growing relationship. All this must be done via SMS, which can be difficult. You get bored in your life at one point or another. This is when you start to look for someone to stimulate and intrigue. Boring people make it difficult to have fun. We want to grow, it gives our self-satisfaction. Partnering with others that can help us accomplish this is what we seek. We want to be the best version of ourselves, and if we have someone along for the ride, then they are the right match. Texting can be a great way to achieve a lot. However, texting should only be used for the beginning stages of a relationship. After you're officially together you'll likely text and Skype every night. In those first texts, what's most important is to be able and willing to send your partner interesting, thought-provoking, and funny texts. This will help you keep your man on his toes. This is why men don't enjoy the old cliche of "Hey or What's Up?". I mean, it's so boring, so easy, and how pointless. Men don't like hearing something so casual. They want to know you care about their lives and ask questions like "How were you at dinner with your dad?" Are you satisfied with the conversation about student loan debt? I'll show you a strategy that will allow you to always be one step ahead and let the tantalizing conversations flow naturally throughout this book.

Because it creates tension, stimulating conversations are important. It makes you more attractive, attractive, and interesting. Attraction creates tension. Even in difficult conversations, you need to show respect. That is how you become someone of consequence. Respect creates value. Respect is the key to maintaining a healthy relationship. Tension is another term for flirting. You can't create an interesting conversation by text. You will need to practice this skill as everyone is different.

However, confidence is essential to get started. He will be devastated if you send him a sassy text after a first date. It could be something like, "If you know what's good for you, he'll give me a call this weekend," or, "If you want to see him in a bathsuit, he should contact me to come hot tubing." This will boost his confidence and make him feel good about spending time with you. This will help him if he is unsure about you. Even though men don't like to be told what should happen, deep down they appreciate not being forced to make decisions. All this confidence will make it difficult for him to keep up and create challenging situations. But be aware that his sassy attitude shouldn't make him seem bossy or smug. Don't forget to compliment your partner. It's a good way to get around the domineering image of a woman he perceives you to be. You can do a lot with compliments. They can help him see the future and think about what they might have. Everyone loves being appreciated. It's easy to make him feel special by a simple text, such as how amazing that shirt looked on him and how sexy that he was able to tell you so much about French wine. Teasing men is a great way to get him to smile. Teasing is great because it focuses in on what's most important in texting. Therefore, the more words the better. It doesn't make sense to write a long book when you can just condense everything into one sentence. There are more opportunities for misinterpretation when you text endlessly. It's possible to use playful teases, such as telling him that something special is on the horizon for him or that he'll pick you up for your next date. It can be playful or cute to tell him that you will see each other again and that when he does it, he will be happy.

Great texting involves great conversation. That is made possible by confidence, creating challenges, making him feel confident through compliments and adding a little spice with a touch of tease. This will guide the relationship in an exciting direction. It will also make you feel more comfortable together because you know that the conversation is real. The relationship can blossom into amazing realms of communication.

Chapter 6: Texting Strategies

Next are some strategies you can use for texting your ex.

Texting your ex is a great way to grab his attention. However, there are certain strategies you can use. You can start by...

1. Reminisce over the good times

You can start by starting with something like this:

Hey, I saw your old battered copy of Lord of the Rings as I was doing some cleaning and all the crazy notes we had at the back. LOL GOOD TIMES

You could also say, "

I was stopped for speeding in an earlier incident. Crazy! Is that the same time we were pulled over in that dingy street?! HAHA

The best thing about this text is its simplicity. Yes, you're reminiscing. However, you aren't being clingy. It happens naturally. Which, of course is the right way for you to move forward with things. When you share that kinda of memory, and with that sort of humor, your ex would feel compelled to answer because he'd feel like talking to someone who's been a big part of him, and not someone who just wants to get out.

It'll be easy for your to start with this text. You can also move to other types of texts, such as playing with jealousy (which will be covered later), or engaging in better conversations.

2. Ask him how he feels.

Next, you might ask your ex how he is doing. This is how to do it:

So how are you? I believe you just started a new job at...wait.

You could also try this:

Was that you I saw at Walgreens on the other night?

It's okay to let him know that you're still watching over him. You will feel more comfortable talking to him if he knows a few details about his life than if he knew everything. This will allow for the conversation to flow naturally.

However, it is wrong to question him about every little thing. It can add a creepy feeling to the conversation. You want him back in your world, not away from it.

3. The jealousy game

Next, you have the option to use the jealousy cards. You don't have be mad or act like he still belongs to you. Keep it subtle, as shown in the image below.

Mike was at my house last week. He mentioned that he saw me with this beautiful girl last month. Hotshot! It was obvious that you had it in you all along!

See? This is a great way to play friend, teasing your friend. When he responds, follow it up with:

Well, I'm pretty sure she's very lucky to have you as her partner!

It will give him some time to realize that if this woman he's seeing is lucky enough to have him then why wouldn't you? It would give him time to consider asking you out again or meeting with you. Which would lead to...

4. The meet-up

If you can successfully complete the three steps above, then he might ask you out. Perhaps you can even ask him out. If he is going to ask you out, your conversation should look like this:

Ex: What's the deal with Saturday night?

You: I had thought about seeing the DiCaprio new film, but I'm not certain...what about you?

Ex. You want to see it together.

You: Yeah, sure, I'd love to. I would let you also know if anything happens, you know.

Ex: So it's a day?

You: HAHA. Mister, you are flirting?

Ex: Maybe.

Continue this process. This is how you create fun and flirty conversations because you never implied any of these things in your previous conversations. This is the way to go if you are going to ask him out.

You: Hey, we'll be around the weekend. Are you looking for a cup of coffee or something else? You could also ask me to bring the book.

Ex: Yeah, sure. I don't think so.

You: Great. I'll be there. For any other questions, please text me.

Ex:

Your advances should be subtle and you might find something that's great.

5. After the date

After you've met up again and have had a productive conversation, you can send him a text the next day. Be gentle, but sweet. Let him know that you enjoyed the date and aren't putting pressure on him. Consider this:

Thanks for having a great night! We should go to something more exciting next time! Xo

It's sweet and enjoyable without all of the pressure. You shouldn't declare your love to someone right away.

6. Talking about yourself

Of course, as time passes, you might start to discuss the status of your relationship and what is next. The one of you who is ready should start. If both of you have gone through the steps with success, he will probably ask you something along the lines of:

So, I thought...wouldn't you love to go on date? It's real! It is just like in the past.

This is where it's important to not immediately say "Yes". You don't want to be an eager beaver. Answer this question:

Are you sure? 100 % sure?

Or:

Did you finally get some sense? LOL NO. You're welcome to, but only if you're certain.

It could be something along those lines. This would let him know you're not as eager but also that you're willing and able to give them two another chance. And that's exactly what your goal is!

Chapter 7: Common Mistakes While Texting

These are the same mistakes I see men make when texting. You can check if you make any of these mistakes in your texting game, and if so, take steps to fix them.

Being Too Emotional

When men text, the number one mistake is appearing too emotional. Most women do not want to add additional drama to their lives or create more problems. Although you may think she sees it as openness and sincerity, it will not be the way she perceives it. Although you may be a great guy, who is honest about his feelings, she does not yet know you.

Before you are able to open your heart to the other person, you must establish a rapport between them. For example, if someone talks to you on the subway about all their problems or their feelings, it is likely to make you feel uncomfortable. If you've only ever met her once in a club, and she does the same thing, it will make you uncomfortable.

Being Too Sexual Too Soon

Some guys are good at being sexual, but you may not be one of them. It is difficult to send sexual text messages to a girl whom you just met, in a way that will get her to respond favorably. It's better to use a lighter, more playful tone. You are likely to drive her away by trying to have too much sexual contact too soon.

If you are able to face rejection and are looking to have a good time, you will be able to go straight to the sexual part.

Even though you may have been able seduce some girls, you'll lose a lot.

Complaining To Her

Won'tful whiners are not liked by anyone. Perhaps you are unhappy at work, don't think you have parents who love you, or your last girlfriend left with your brother. You don't have to tell your girlfriend about this. Your perception of yourself will reflect the quality of your life. If you can tell her about the amazing things going on in your life, she will view you as interesting. If, on the other side, you're constantly complaining about the things in your life that aren't so great, then she might also see you as the same.

Even if she doesn't feel so good about herself, she probably won't be interested in a party of pity. Instead, encourage her to see the positives in life and show her how it can be fun. It doesn't mean that you shouldn't share your problems with her. It is also a bad idea to talk about your past experiences with women. It is not attractive to indicate that you have had a string of bad relationships.

Being Needy

This is a huge error and most likely more common than any other mistake on this list. The problem with this is that it's completely normal. We want to get to know someone we like. Texting is extremely easy. Just a few keystrokes are all it takes to send a simple text.

Problem is, if you send too much or too little text messages, you will make her feel needy. You can also ask her questions about what she is up to. You might find occasions when this approach works. There are times when the connection might be real and she will love the attention you place on her. You will most likely make her feel stressed and drive her away. You should allow the relationship time to develop naturally. Give her some space.

You shouldn't use humor in your texts

You'll see many girls using "hehehe" and "ha ha" in texts. This text should not be copied. LOL emoticons and any other emoticons are fine because they soften the harshness of teasing. Humor in a conversation is strictly a girl thing. Women enjoy a man who is funny. Even though he wasn't the most handsome man, you have likely seen him or heard of someone who loved his humor. You could see him laughing out loud and making funny jokes. Have you ever seen successful pickups where the women were making jokes and the men couldn't stop laughing? It doesn't happen, and it shouldn't be in your texts.

Acting Jealous

When you meet a girl for the first time and get her number, it is important to realize that she is not committed. Even if she has slept in your bed until she tells you that she will not see anyone else, you aren't obligated to her. Therefore, you shouldn't be unrealistic in your expectations of her faithfulness.

Her possible relationships with other guys doesn't make her an easy or attractive sexy sexy. Naturally, jealousy can set in if your dream girl sees other guys. Because men are territorial by nature, they won't share what they see with other guys. You will look jealous, and she will leave you.

But that doesn't mean you shouldn't try to play around with it. It doesn't matter if she has a boyfriend. Then we come to the idea for testing.

What to do when she tests you

There is a phrase called a "shit test" in the world of pickup. A shittest involves a girl making a provocative or rude gesture to a man to test his ability to handle it. A man who is confident in himself will not be bothered and be able to respond or joke about the test.

Perhaps she will do one of these rude shittests in a text chat. You might also find her bringing up the fact that she is going on a date. Your response to this could make a huge difference in how she views your character. If, for instance, she mentions that she is seeing someone and you are not bothered by it, then this will make her naturally curious.

She will wonder what it means that you are so unconcerned about her being with someone else. Consider actors and rock stars who are known for sleeping with numerous women. They wouldn't be surprised if one of their groupies was having an affair with another guy. They don't need women to claim their rights, they know that they have the ability to get another man. Because this type of confidence seems rare, it's highly appealing.

How Often should you text her?

If you are texting a girl who you haven't yet slept with, there is a golden rule: you shouldn't double-text. A double message is one that you send to another girl before she replies to the first. The same way we may sometimes make women double-text in order to gauge her interest level, double-texting is a sign that we love her too much.

There are exceptions to every rule. This rule is important until you're able to text consistently well and feel confident. Even though double-texting may seem appealing at times, there will be occasions when it is not. Perhaps you are wondering if your text is being misinterpreted. You may also believe that your text has been misunderstood.

Sorry, bud. You'll have to try again. It is extremely unlikely that your first message hasn't reached her. Even if you try to clarify things to get her to understand, it won't help. You will come across as desperate. It is important to wait for the woman to respond to your text message before sending it out. If a woman doesn't answer a message you send, it is likely she isn't interested. Let it go, and move on to something else.

You don't have the right to abandon her. It should be left for around a week before you send another text. Don't refer to the first text. Just send a funny text about something you are doing. You might be able to restart the conversation. If she doesn't reply, it's probably time to stop following. She's clearly not interested, so pursuing her will only make you a stalker.

You shouldn't be too serious when writing texts

If you have serious things to say, then texting is not the best medium. It's best to be casual and lighthearted when you first start a relationship. Wait until you've gotten to know your partner before discussing your personal lives or expectations. These serious conversations should not take place via text.

Texting can't express the feelings you have or be accurate in expressing them. The more complicated the message, the easier it will be to misunderstand. If you feel the need to speak up about something serious, either call her at her place of business and let her hear your thoughts or wait until she sees you face to face. If the topic is very serious, you can leave it until you are ready to discuss it.

You shouldn't text with certain conversations. Perhaps she's been seeing other guys, and you don't like it. If this is the case, you should meet with her face to face and discuss your expectations for the relationship. Perhaps you are looking to date other people. Talking to her face-to-face about this topic is important. Perhaps you are confused about where your relationship is headed and want to clarify it again. Call her or come and see her.

This is counterproductive. If you're not seeing each other in person and texting is your only way of communicating, you should seriously reconsider whether this is a relationship you want to have. A real relationship is one in which you regularly see each others in person. Texting is only the beginning of a real relationship.

The Art of Intimacy

To create intimacy, you can simply assume it already exists. By this I mean that you think about the way you communicate with your friends while texting them. Because they already know you, you probably won't send them a "What are you interested in doing for fun?" text. If you ask these kinds of questions or act too formal, you create space between yourself and the women who you are texting.

You are assuming that there is some kind of relationship between you two by being playful and using a nickname.

Another way is to refer to something that happened between you, like "Those girls who were fighting, insane!" This will help you establish that you are not strangers.

Be a copycat

An old saying states that opposites attract. This saying, however, isn't as valid as many other old sayings. People prefer people who are like them. There are exceptions to this rule, but for most people it is easier and more effective to build attraction with someone who feels the same way as you.

Look at the way she writes when you get a text from a girl you are interested in. Do you see her using words often? How long are her text messages? Are her texts friendly or more formal? In your response, you can incorporate elements from her texting style with you own. It doesn't mean you have to write exactly the same way she does. You could look weird, especially if your writing style is very feminine. However, it is important to try to match her style.

This is why it is so important. Imagine you were attending a high-end dinner party, and you were dressed in shorts with a t-shirt and flip-flops. While everyone at the party is educated and speaks in a formal tone, you constantly use slang. It is possible that, while you may enjoy the party, you won't fit into the group.

The only thing I will say is that even though she may shorten a lot of words and her spelling skills are poor, it doesn't mean that I would do the same thing. Be less formal in your writing, but avoid making mistakes. While it is good to include elements of her style within your texts, this should not be done if it violates any other rules.

Chapter 8: Mindset To Text Success

Positive thinking is key

As with everything in life, you need the right mindset to succeed. Texting should be avoided if you feel anxious, sad, pressured, or rushed. You're more likely to make mistakes if your mood is not good.

Boredom can lead to boring texts, which will make girls feel bored, ask boring questions and result in zero results. You will lose girls if you send them messages out of desperation, lack of wealth, and neediness. Keep positive things happening in your life and keep a positive attitude.

Unless youre in the middle of messaging with a girl and are trying to make plans, waiting to reply to her message will not cause you any harm. However, you could be hurt by one really bad SMS. Don't send a message if you're not sure of the content. You can't get it back once you have hit send.

Get ready to act

It is your responsibility to ask the girl out. Chances are she will not ask or make any effort to meet you. In order to get results you will have to be in control. This means that you will be the one to guide her through the entire interaction, from the first text she sends to add value in her life to the final message and the closing. You must assume that she will follow you on that journey. Sometimes showing that you can be the guy who does those things is enough to attract her.

Patience

As we have said before, girls need to feel comfortable and safe before being willing to meet up with you. This takes patience. Sometimes slow is the fastest way to get her on date. If you speed up and get a 'No,' it's likely that you'll be slowing her down. Better to ask her out via three texts and get yeses.

Persistence

You must be persistent if you want to get results. If she's clearly not comfortable with you and rejects you, then you should terminate the relationship.

It is easy to see this on text messages and apps. Girls will first reject you by unmatching with you or blocking your number if they aren't interested.

You can revive the conversation by adding value, even if a girl doesn't respond. While a girl may not yet be convinced about you, she will know that you are the one who made the decision.

Persistence and perseverance are key. In certain situations, your persistence can be considered attractive.

Persistence isn't only for one girl. Persistence is crucial throughout the entire texting process with any girl.

Chapter 9: How to send a first text message to a girl.

The Internet has revolutionized the world. It is no longer necessary to call a girl to invite them on a date. You can meet almost everyone online, just think of all the different dating sites. All conversations take place via SMS. No matter if you meet a girl in school, at a club, or at a pub, all your subsequent conversations will be via text. There are many online chat options, but WhatsApp is the most common. It doesn't matter which chat app you use online, but you must be a good texter if you want your crush not to just be a crush.

You want to learn how you can make a girl like yours over text. After all, if she likes what you do over text, she will likely like you in real-life.

Although texting may not be as scary as making a phone calls, it's still quite an art. There are many unspoken rules about texting. Some rules of texting girls are very simple. Never use the letter 'k, otherwise the girl will think that you aren't interested in her. While others are more complicated.

I will simplify the rules and give you a few ideas to think about. You will also learn all the secrets to getting a date with that girl you want.

Texting a girl should be fun, polite, and kind. While respect is essential, it's also important to show interest in your girl. This is not a texting conversation about an office meeting, it is about possibility. It's about the possibility of love, dating, and future romance. While it is important to be respectful, you must also show that you care. It's important not to show too much interest, as you might be frightening the pretty girl. Be respectful, polite, and kind while still flirtatious.

Be yourself.

Let's say that you know a girl. Perhaps you have seen her only once, or just once.

You think she's amazing but you don't know if you even exist. You have a crush and a suspicion that she may have a crush. You can't help but think about her. Her beauty, personality, and popularity are all amazing. Part of you feels that she won't be interested as you because you're not an "it" guy. Another part of you feels it would foolish to not give it a try. You're not going to text her as that would be too awkward.

Be friendly and polite when you text her. You should be you from the beginning.

Be yourself and you will be able learn to make a girl love you. You don't need to be bravo and all macho. Instead, be real. Real men are more attractive to girls, regardless of gender. These are some of the things you can do in your first texts.

Say hi to her in a friendly and casual manner. Be friendly and flirtatious.

Do not wait to text her if she meets you at a bar or at a party. There was a ridiculous idea of waiting for her to respond so you don't appear too keen.

Hell, no! If you have already met her and found her attractive, you can send her an instant text. It was a pleasure to meet her.

If it's a blind date then introduce yourself, tell her her number and give a little bit about yourself to avoid making you look like a complete stranger. Finally, tell her that you would like to meet her.

These things are flexible depending on the crush you have, if she is already your friend, and what you are trying to achieve. You don't have to be strict or fast. Just keep it brief and respectful. Also, let her know you like her. Let her know that you would love to meet up with her.

The rules are the next section! These rules are important to understand. Let's imagine that you have sent one of the previous texts to her. You might have to write a few more sentences. You have hit the send key and are now waiting to hear back from her. These rules are key to success:

Do not wait on the phone for a reply. You could end up driving yourself crazy by waiting. You can do something once you've pressed send. You can take a walk, watch Netflix, or go to the fitness center.

Don't send her a second text at once. Give her plenty of time to respond. It might take her an hr, an hour or two hours to respond. You may need to wait for at least a day before sending another message.

If she does no reply to your first message, you can still send her another one. It's possible to do it 24 hours later than the original. The second text should not be overly formal. Keep it lighthearted and funny. Use humor and flirtatious language in your texting.

If she responds, it's just amazing. Then you can have more text conversations and learn to text girls without being annoying.

These are just a few examples for first-time texts.

"Susan, it's James. I made a positive impression on you when we met last night. I would like to talk to you and find out more about you.

"Molly. Hey, this David. Matthew Price is a good friend. He suggested that I call him. We're both Yale students, and he thinks we're compatible. Would you be interested in chatting?

"Hi Martha. While you may not be my friend, at least, I do not think so. We have many mutual friends online. We are both in philosophy classes, which I find very difficult. I'm located in Greenpoint.

The texts above are formal, polite and friendly but not too flirtatious. It is better not to flirt with someone until there have been a few exchanges of texts. However, if you feel you must be flirtatious from beginning, then you can try:

"Susan. This is James. We met at a party last night, and I have to admit that you left the most amazing impression on us. It's hard not to think about you."

"Molly I know it is exam time, and you are probably frantically studying. I saw you at football last evening, but only briefly. I hope you are still with me. I'd love to meet you again.

"Martha. We are mutual friends at university. I have seen you around, and I am so impressed with you! We would love to meet. This is Matt.

All the texts above contain a touch of politeness, respect, good grammar, spelling, fun, and flirtatiousness. It is not acceptable to have sweethearts or babies. If you are excessively sexy or exaggerated, the girl will go a mile. But that is just the beginning.

Chapter 10: Get his attention with a text

Although texting isn't as effective at attracting women than in-person meetings, it is still a good way to get out of your comfort zone. You can also use it to motivate him to have more dates.

With all that said, texting is an effective method to attract a man and keep his attention.

10 Steps for Strategic Texting that Will Build Attraction

This section of this guide will talk about texting strategies, steps, and other ways to attract men.

#1: Always start with casual

It is tempting to become text-crazy after you exchange your phone numbers with a man that you like.

Understanding that you are not helping your cause by doing so is crucial. Over-texting him right after getting his number can be counterproductive. It will make you seem eager to get with him' which is likely going to cause him to lose interest. Men's attraction to women is built on the thrill and excitement of the chase. He will not feel attracted if it isn't as though he is actively pursuing you, tempting you, or winning you over.

You can start casually by exchanging phone numbers and capturing the attention of a man you are interested in. Do not let him text first.

You can also text him something casual, such as: "Hey, passing bus banner advertising toothpaste just reminded mich of your sweet smiling."

You can send him something casual to spark a conversation.

#2: Move beyond "Hi!" clichés

They may have fallen short of what they deserve, but modern women have become so lazy that they don't even text "hi!" when texting a man they love and whose attention is theirs.

The intention of the "hi" message is to establish a conversation by prompting him to inquire about you. He would give you his number if he did not know. But, such a lazy text message cannot capture the attention and respect of a man just like you who is as well-equipped as you.

Do more than just send him a text saying "hi" to get his attention. He will appreciate your thoughtfulness and giving you something to communicate.

The example text is used to create and send a text message to him that is encouraging, prodding and complimentary. Because we are talking about complimenting his work:

#3: Compliment text will take you far

Look at the example text message that was highlighted in the first stage. You'll notice that it's casual in tone and intended to spark a conversation. However, the message also contains a subtle, or perhaps not so subtle, compliment.

A common misconception is that men don't appreciate compliments. This is true even though it is very popular among empowered women. Men appreciate compliments equally as women, if not more, so sending a text message to compliment him, or a text message in which you give a genuine compliment, is a good idea. This is the logic.

If you are a confident, powerful, and beautiful woman, you will probably get many compliments every day from men. Do you know how many compliments beautiful women get from the man who is interested in you? A text message with a genuine compliment is more effective than sending him a text message.

Be gentle and playful, not too much. He will likely follow your cues because the excitement at being complimented by someone as beautiful as you is will fuel his desire and drive him to chase after you.

#4: Flirty texts will send flutters into his heart

The next step builds on the one before it.

There is a chance that you will start a conversation by texting him a compliment. This is good, because you can use text to build intimacy in his head and heart.

Begin by starting to text him about casual topics. Then, start to read his cues. Finally, build your way towards texting him flirtatious messages. This is the same as what you would do when meeting in-person.

Texting with him shows that although you are successful and a woman of high standards, you also have feminine qualities and can tap into your feminine energy to make men feel valued.

You should never send him a flirtatious SMS message straight away. Instead build up to it.

#5 - Banter texts are never a failure

Banter is a playful and friendly exchange with teasing remarks. Banter texts add to the conversation and drive it forward.

They are a lot of flirtatious messages. However, they are substantive and based only on the replies from the man you like.

Banter works best when it is done in person. But, you can still use it to attract him over text. By way of example, you could initiate a roleplay scenario through your text correspondence. He will be open to you sharing information about what you like and dislike about romantic love.

#6 - Unavailability is attractive

One of the things that we have discussed is that men like the thrill of the chase. A man who feels that he has work to get your attention --there are limits-- will feel more attracted to you.

Many women make the mistake, though, of not being available to respond to their husband's texts. There is a time for it. After establishing a romantic relationship with someone, most couples go through a period of texting or chatting. It is normal to reply to his messages.

You should also not reply to all his messages at once. This will make him feel like you're always waiting for him text so that you can reply.

It is not a game of mind if you do not reply immediately to his text. It is more a strategic way of increasing your attractiveness.

It is important to note how fast he responds. If he responds quickly, it's a sign that he's really into you. This is why you should respond in your own way. If he takes longer to reply, you should wait a little longer. You could even text something that shows he has a busy lifestyle.

You could text him "Hey stranger," if you get a text from your friend just as you're about to go out for a girls' evening or a meeting. We are happy to talk to you. I'm going into___ (tell him what you're doing). Do you want to chat?

As you can see from the text, it will signal that you're busy with your own life. He won't be distracted by you pinning for attention. This will grab his attention and make him more attracted to you.

#7 - Purposeful texts will grab his attention

If you are an empowered, successful woman, and have high standards for yourself, you shouldn't be following a man who lacks the motivation and drive to accomplish amazing things with her life.

We assume that the man who attracts your attention is a motivated and purposeful man. Otherwise, you will be shortchanging yourself.

Attracting the right man is not about sending him text messages for fun. You want him to be driven and purposeful, so don't just send him messages to get a kick out of it. Send him text messages to help you drive towards a goal, what we call purposeful texts messages.

You want to get to understand him and make plans for the future. This will allow you to keep your time valuable. He will feel respected.

#8 - Show your interest in asking questions

Only a woman who asks questions that are interesting will draw a man's attention. Consider it this:

How does it make a woman feel to be asked interesting questions by a man they like? Does that not speak volumes about his genuine interest in you and your hobbies? It does. It does the same thing for you.

It doesn't matter if you are the one who initiates a conversation via SMS or he is the one who takes the initiative, make sure your messages contain interesting questions about the person receiving them.

You could, for example, mention that he had an important conference to attend. At the end of the day or when you feel certain that he has finished the meeting, send him an SMS message with the following: "Hey handsome. How was the meeting?

Showing interest in his lives will make him feel valued. That will get his attention and create an attraction that will lead to his response in kind.

#9 - Abbreviated Texts are a big Turn Off

Abbreviating text messages is one of the most common mistakes made in texting by women. Abbreviating text messages can be annoying, especially for men who are busy with their own goals and do not have the time to decipher them.

Additionally, it is easy to be sophomoric by abbreviating texts messages, especially if the abbreviations don't make sense or are hard to understand immediately. For example, @TEOTD and LMK.

Most smartphones come with dictionary autocomplete, which makes it quick and easy to type in a word. If you are not roleplaying a spygame and trying send each other cryptic texts messages, texting your friend like a teenager is a waste of time.

Use abbreviations wherever necessary -- a LOL here, there, is OK -- but don't go overboard.

#10: The secret is simple and sweet

Now that you have successfully attracted his attention, your interest and attraction through the above steps, don't succumb to the temptation for him to read texts that are similar to novels.

It is important to keep text messages short and sweet if you want to catch his attention or build sexual attraction. You can tease your date with witty banter, if you are trying to tell him something very deep or that will require more words, You won't get any results by texting him long messages.

Sending a text message is not the best way to communicate with someone you don't want to be out with. Instead, send a voicemail. He will be grateful for your thoughtfulness and will likely appreciate it.

It shows respect for his time by writing short texts.

Note: You should also be careful not to send unstructured text messages (or even two-worded) all the time. You will appear uninterested and these texts can be detrimental to your career.

Once you have gained his attention and his attraction, you must maintain it. Next, you will learn valuable texting strategies that will make it easier to do this successfully.

Chapter 11: Attracting with Texts

It is easy to attract a guy by texting. Try to be interesting while not being too obvious.

You should be funny and witty. Clever, yet not silly.

He may not always be right. I get that you want him not to agree with everything you say. However, you will be more successful if you challenge him. Males are bored and unattractive to pushovers who do not have an opinion.

Keep him guessing. You might not want to answer a text message within a few seconds of it being received. Wait until the next business day to answer another. You shouldn't expect him to be consistent. If he expects to be able to text you every day at 10:30, he will take it as a given and become bored.

Be a little bit assertive. Be a little more direct than he expects. If he teases and you respond, tease back.

Flirting feels like ping-pong or chess. The tension comes from the back and forth between equal sides. If one team has all the power, then the game becomes boring. There must be a balance between both sides.

The attraction will begin to fade when the balance is tilted too far in one direction.

It's not hard to do. All you have to do is what we've discussed throughout the guide.

Text him once more, but don't send another one until he replies. Texting him endlessly will not make you more or less interested.

Let's take, for instance:

Mike: Hey! What are your thoughts? (This is an inexcusable way to start a message. You shouldn't do this. However, you should be prepared as it is the beginning text most guys use.

You: We are just trying to find a cure. (You did not say "not enough" or another boring response like he would expect.

Mike: lol. How is that going?

It might take another seven days. You were just thinking about me. He was. He just texted to you!

Mike: How did you get that information?

You: I was once a psychic.

Then you should follow this text by adding another, which will say;

You: You'd probably be shocked at how much I know about YOU!

Okay, you get it. It's not necessary to reply with the same old material that everyone else has sent. Don't be afraid to go a little crazy. Instead of sending him the same tired text messages, other girls can send him something different. You could be the one he actually enjoys hearing from because it is what you are writing to him.

Chapter 12: Captain her ship of emotions

We are now entering the final section of mastering text. To turn her on, use specific words.

Do yourself a favor. This concept is something I strongly believe in. You can visit amazon's kindle stores right now. You will find romance novels at 75% of the top sellers.

Why?

BECAUSE IT'S PORNED TO GIRLS

I would highly recommend you visit the free section to download a copy of a top-selling romance novel for free. You can then see professional word play.

They don't like these bullshit stories where a guy sweeps a girl off of her feet.

Romance novels writers use extremely descriptive key terms to hook readers' heads and give them an emotional orgasm.

I was a marketer so I knew all about romance novels. To find out if those principles could lead to a woman falling in love with you, I read several of the books. The answer is yes.

This is the key, however, to not come off as too strong too soon. If you are texting someone, or have had a sexual encounter in person, you should try to apply these tactics.

Concept #1: Sexual Terms - Women Also have Dirty Minds

I have no idea why men think women should be considered non-human. The mentality of every man is that they will tiptoe to the side and pretend that she has an evil intention. Do you think you could keep tip toeing for ever?

Then, the guys realize that the girls are finally getting the point of the tip toeing and start thinking "oh my shit she has onto me fuck", assuming that it is her calling you out.

Instead of looking at it like you're teeinging until she gives you the signal, shift your mindset to follow her. Baby is an important step towards building trust in the relationship and moving it forward at the right speed. She will give you a shot if she thinks you are a good guy. But, to make her trust you, get to understand you, and see you in different situations, she will need to first build a relationship.

The tip-toe mentality must be broken and girls should realize that they want sex just like men.

Because her mind is just so dirty, finding clever ways for her to add sexual terms will get... you guessed...sexual thoughts.

"I'll send to you the pic of the crazy lady I saw at sex today."

"Woops in for a sex."

"Wtf does autocorrect do?"

"sec"

"finally"

She is reading a text that you sent, meaning she is thinking about it. She is also seeing the term SEX THREE TIMES.

It seems that everything leads to the next, and the woman's mind is racing. You are not a creep, and you have succeeded in not coming off as such.

"You'll be proud to hear that I finally got this haircut"

"I always leave my man Steve a great tie"

"fuck tit"

"TIP"

"wow"

Another idiotic example, "FUCKTIT", and her mind wanders to other things. She might find it hilarious and make a joke of it.

Think about it. Sexual thoughts + laughter = floodgates open to accept and receive sexual thoughts. Thoughts you shared with her.

You + Funny + Sex is what her brain is processing.

Words can be very powerful for men!

One amazing trick you can do is to begin a statement by using "my friend" (or "this man"). This gives you so much power that it is almost ridiculous. You are free to say anything you want. This takes away your responsibility and allows you to say what you want. You can still stimulate those sexual feelings.

It's the best thing, a lot of girls who hear'my friend" will guess a little and then think back and forth on whether it's actually you. Unless you give a name to a friend, she will probably spend more time pondering whether or not it is you.

Here is an example.

"Hey, I'd like to know something about my friend. Instagram is what he loves the most. He claimed that it is a girl's favorite thing.

He says: "My friend just told me something, and I felt the need to tell you. But I don't know how you would handle it."

Her: "What does it mean? It is not difficult to handle haha

He said, "He said the girl that he is going out to with wanted him doing that scene from 50 shades. It's the one where he drinks the wine and then kisses her. He should do it.

Concept #2: Engineer Her Subconscious

This is where you can playfully use language to get her thinking.

Let's say you and a woman shared the same cup or chap stick.

You: "There's not hiding it"

Her: "What?"

You: "I am sure that you chewed your chap stick upon returning home"

You:

I bolded soft & perfect because she will subconsciously think about your lips. She is not thinking about mowing your lawn... SHE THINKS ABOUT KISSING You!

Alright. If you haven't done so, it's now time to ACT. We live in an amazing time when you can practice this stuff with random women you've never met on Tinder or Instagram.

Your text game will be adjusted to your personal preferences. I know that some of you have read this to improve your text game and help you get one girl. You may just be looking for a friend. Texting other women is not a good idea unless you are already in a relationship.

It will increase your social skills exponentially. You'll make new friends, build confidence and gain more respect from her. It is important to remember that women will judge you based on how many times you have been pre-approved by other women.

This will force your boundaries and allow you to make changes. Try to accomplish 'x amount' of numbers in as little time as possible. Beginners should aim to reach 10 solid numbers in just 14 days. Limit your online resources to only 3-4.

Chapter 13: Getting the Love Machine in Gear With Sexting

First Gear: Warming up the engine and shifting it into Flirty first gear

Here are some examples of sexy texts to help you get from a flirty first gear into high-speed racing mode. These sexts are sure to set the mood for your date and spark his imagination.

Second Gear: Make Your Sex Life More Sexy by Putting Your Life into Second Gear

Men Love the Wrapper and The Present Inside

Men can be extremely visual. They enjoy the wrapper especially if they know what the prize inside is. Here is a suggestion for couples shopping. Grab the Victoria's Secret catalogue and order some lingerie online.

Eye candy may get him interested in your outfit that night. Or it might give you some insight into his style preferences so that you can put on a fabulous wrapper for another night. Then, you'll see him happy when you unwrap that beautiful package that is you!

Here are some sexy texts that you can use for him to recall the lingerie talk you had.

"Can I help a sister out -- what should I put on from my collection of lingerie?"

"If you are worthy I will show the lingerie, beyond sexy!"

If you get in the shower together, it is okay to get a little dirt.

Somebody once said that sex only becomes dirty if it's done well. As you get closer to each other, you'll be able engage in more explicit sexual talk. Here are some examples.

"If you heard me tell you what my thoughts were, you would blush!"

"We can use the whippedcream I bought for dessert."

"There are certain places I just can't reach with my Love Lotion -- can You help me?"

"I remember a song I used to sing today: 'When you think about me, I touch yourself.'"

Men are visual. So paint a picture about how hot it's going to get.

Men love to imagine sexual scenarios. Here are some examples to spark his curiosity:

"I'm taking a survey. Do you prefer to be at the top or bottom?"

"Rest up. Tonight, you are going for a workout."

"I heard an old tune: 'Show Me, Show Me How You Do That Thing. She said ...'".

"Is he wrong for me want you this bad?"

"Not to put pressure on you, but... get ready be sweaty tonight."

Third Gear: Building a Head Of Steam

"I want your bang on me like a hurricane screen door."

"Here's the thing that's going on when you get home. It is going be hot, it's getting sweaty, and it is getting sexy. Get out there and stretch -- I don't want to see you pulling a muscle."

"The women magazine in the supermarket claims that there are five different ways to make men reach their ultimate climax. Can you guess how many we can do tonight?"

Here are some hilarious and sexy sexts to send to set the mood

"Tonight I ask that you tell me if I'm interested in a position, what position should I take?"

"I want your hands to be filled with my arse and you to make pizza dough out of it!"

"I am taking an online survey: Would you like a hug first, a kiss, or do you prefer to go straight up to the Nasty?"

"Not to put pressure on you...but if I don't have you within me tonight I will be so unhappy... can we help a little girl out?"

"Old tune: "How deep are your loves?" and it made you think of me.. and all your parts / junk/ tools/ dick.

"Tell Me What Makes You Hard... Go ahead, I won't blush ..."

"Tonight I want you and your partner to slap my shins as if we were playing ping pong!"

"If I bring the balls, you'll get the net for them to stuff in!"

Fourth gear: The Sexy Speed Limit

These ideas will get his engine revving.

"I can play any hole ..." like a par-3.

"When you think of the things you are going to make me do, I get all wet ..."

"I love to be on all fours. I look over my shoulder and see you. Happy ..."

"I'm going pop you like a champagne cork!" !"

"What about if we played hide and seek -- I can hide your dickin in you. Which hole are you going to use first?

"I am going ride you like I'm a pony tonight."

"I'm texting to you with one handed, but the second is very busy getting ready ..."

"You are inside my head ..."

Chapter 14: Keep her interested in your texts

Although it may be easy to capture her interest initially, they will soon become bored. It is possible for women to get used the monotony of your texts and lose interest in dating you. Here are some tips to keep the flames of desire ablaze.

Find a way that you can remain mysterious. You don't have to divulge everything. You don't have to tell the girl everything.

You can also let her wait before replying to her message. The longer she waits, she is more curious and more interested.

You shouldn't give her a nickname that is too long. Sometimes, you can just call her by the real name. Tell her how sexy and fitting her name is. It's easy to find a complimenting adjective to her name. For example, Isabelle sounds great. It's so sensual, it suits me."

Be consistent in your texting approach. She may expect a specific type of text when it arrives in a certain style. Be playful at times, and humorous or mysterious at others. Take care not to be confused for someone with multiple personality disorder.

You should never text her because you are bored. Even if you're just texting to pass time, she could pick it up. Women have an unexplainable power of intuition and gut-feel.

You can spice up the conversation by using emoticons, funny videos, audio clips, and photos. Send her something that you think will remind her of you.

These can serve to be a good topic for the two of you.

It's okay to express your feelings for her, but you shouldn't go into too many details. You can remind her how unique she is without being too pompous or insincere.

After you have started dating, you can drive her back to her house and send her something sweet like "Thanks for the love." It was a great evening. All it takes to make someone fall in love is a little sweetness or sincerity.

It's also important to let her see you occasionally. You both can take a rest and enjoy it. It can make her miss you even more and encourage her to get in touch with you again. As the old saying goes: "Absence does indeed make the heart fonder."

Chapter 15: How to Keep Multiple Women Happy at the Same Time

Texting has the advantage of allowing you to communicate with multiple girls at one time. Text messaging is great for guys who want to communicate with multiple girls or just want to be open to new possibilities.

Texting can be a great way of keeping in touch with girls you're interested in. If a woman replies to a message you send, it is a great way to bring yourself in front of her eyes. If your message is funny or flirtatious (which it should be), then she will associate the messages from you with a pleasant experience.

It doesn't take too long to send messages to the girls listed in your phonebook. Even if you are messaging multiple girls, it is important to follow the rules. Be sure to not send boring "hey what's the up" texts. Be lighthearted and tell her what you're up to or how something reminds you of you.

Send another text to one of your other girls after you've sent them the first one. This way, you can stay connected with at least five girls in just a few minutes. I suggest that you use these text messages when you are on the go, such as while you wait at Starbucks for your coffee. You will communicate spontaneity and show you are a busy guy.

You don't need permission

Men who text women to ask them out on dates will usually first ask permission. You may be wondering what I mean. It's not common for a man to send a text asking a woman out, then then sending a follow up text asking her again.

You can ask permission to say:

"Does this sound like something you would love to do?"

"Would you love to go to movies?"

"Are your Saturdays free?"

You can ask her to go out, but you need her permission. Your request is not confident and almost sounds like a beggar. It's almost as if she wanted to do you a favor by saying yes.

Asking a girl out in this manner gives her ample opportunity to decline. It's not difficult for girls to decide whether they want to go out on their own, so why not start by asking her "Are you available next Saturday?"

If she answers, "Sorry, but I'm spending the night with my family," then you are in an awkward spot. She may ask you again "How about Friday, then?" This will be seen as being needy. This is basically saying you don't live a normal life and have no plans on Saturday or Friday.

Although she may be genuinely interested in you, she may also be doing something with family on Saturday. You have now closed the door on any chance to get more information. If she is unsure if she wants you to date her, you can basically focus on telling her to say no.

It is important to not make the first date too much of a commitment when you ask a girl out. For example do a Thursday day night date. Thursday indicates that you have plans to go on Friday and Saturday. This gives you perceived social value. It's unlikely that she will be doing anything on Thursday, so you won't be turned away.

Another option is to make arrangements for the date in advance of when you want to meet up with your friends. You could mention in your message that you're going to meet with your friends later on. Would she be interested in meeting up for a drink prior? This is great because it removes some of her fears about you being creepy. This artificial time constraint means she knows she won't be able spend any more time with you if it doesn't suit her. It's also not suggested that the date will lead any other activity, i.e. sex. This is a way to create status. It shows your friends that you enjoy fun activities.

Removing some of the pressure will help her make a commitment to you. If your date is going well, ask her if it would be a good idea to invite your friends. If you're the kind of guy who loves to move a relationship along quickly, then you should consider making location changes for your date.

This refers to the notion that time is essentially perceptual. You are likely to have felt the time seem to fly by. You must feel that sufficient time has passed before most women will consent to sleeping with your partner. This is the traditional no sex after the first date rule.

To overcome this rule, you can either agree with her standards about when it is okay to have sexual activity by setting up enough dates. You can either make enough location changes so that it feels like you have spent much time together. Moving her from one place to the next will reduce the time you spend waiting before you can make your first move.

If you really think about it, this is even more apparent. If you take a woman out to a bar, spend an hour talking to her, and then try to kiss them within that hour, most likely she will turn you down unless you are a master seducer. But if you can get her out of the bar and into something more, like a house party or a Karaoke evening with your friends, or even watching your friends' band at a jazz venue, then getting physical with her will become a natural part of the night.

You create the impression of being together a lot. You can relate this to the first question: "Would you like to go to bar with me?" Later we could have a drink at a local bar, then later we could visit a jazz club to see my friend play, and maybe even karaoke late into the night. There's a good possibility she'll turn you down. You have asked her too many commitments at once.

But if you offer to take her out for just a few drinks, with no strings attached then she will likely say yes. It doesn't mean that you have to end the date. You can plan where you'll take her the rest of the night. This plan is best if you both enjoy each others company. If she doesn't match your expectations, then there is an easy way out.

You shouldn't try to make her happy.

Pick up artists tend to emphasize flaws and imperfections in women. You could point out that her hands are large or that you have seen another girl wearing the same outfit she is wearing that same night. This will help to break down her "Bitch Shield" as well as undermine her confidence. This is a powerful technique for approaching attractive women.

Texting can be more efficient, but it is not as effective. The fact that it is written makes it seem less like a casual comment and more serious. It is likely that these will be used in a text to insult a girl. This illustrates how much damage can be done by using a combination of techniques that work for one situation but don't work in another.

While being playful and teasing will work well with your texts, be aware of crossing the line. You can also include emoticons in your message to soften it. :-) Or;-) If you tease her, take a look at the message before you send it. Make sure that you aren't teasing or insulting. You can make a big difference in her response.

Lead her down the Path

The most important aspect of texting is to think strategically. Many men will text randomly, with no clear purpose. Better to think strategically and get her on the right path to accepting you as a date partner.

Moving down a particular path is more effective than asking her for help out of nowhere. This is because it is less abrupt. Imagine you were having a good conversation with your boss about a small matter and suddenly the bomb exploded on you. They are changing the company. You will now have a completely different title and set of job responsibilities.

This news is likely to shock you. While you might not react in the best way, or vice versa, suddenly everything is different. You can imagine instead that you knew about these changes weeks ahead of time. This was because you were already familiar with the idea of the new position and the change felt more subtle.

You are not creating an environment that allows you to suddenly ask "Do you want go out with me?" You can lead her down a route where she will feel comfortable agreeing to the date.

Start by asking her if you are more into jazz music or indie. It is best to not ask her a question like, "What music do you enjoy?". That will put you in interview mode. Her answer will dictate how you ask for her out. If she is a fan of indie music, you could say something like, "then you'll be a great friend's musician, he's playing next Wednesday, I'll pick her up at 7 to take you there." If Jazz music is what she enjoys, you could offer her a date.

Also, it is not necessary to ask her to go out with them. Instead, assume that she will accept your choice of language. This gives you confidence and increases the likelihood that she will accept your language. Asking someone a question is a way to force them into answering your questions. She doesn't have to answer a question if you offer an option. It's always the easiest option.

Chapter 16: Flirtexting Vs Sexting

It's not about sexting. Yes, sexting can be fun if both of you are into it. However, this should not be done in the beginning stages of a relationship. You want to get to understand each other without having to worry about sexual messaging or inappropriate pictures.

By skipping the flirtexting step in favor of casual texting and sexting, it is possible that you are being a bootycall.

Sexting is acceptable. However, flirtexting sends a very different message. Sexting isn't about building something lasting with someone.

What Flirtexting Can Do for Your Relationship

Flirting is a great way to get started in a relationship. It is a way to hint at a little spice and suggest that things will get friendlier.

Flirting is a way to signal that things have finally picked up. For a long-standing relationship, flirtexting can be the catalyst to rekindle the passion that was once intense.

It doesn't matter how old the relationship or how recent it is. What matters most is how you both respond to the messages. Flirting can be done if you are sending messages and have someone in your mind.

Flirtexting is using the Language of Love and Not NASA

Oh hai. We haz probz now. Lol!

The last "sentence", as a text, arrived and you're scratching your heads wondering what it might be. Sorry to disappoint, but you just got a text message. This text was sent by one of the hardcore messagers who forgot that humans are people and that we love words.

Let me say, "Oh hi. We have a problem. (Laugh out Loud). The phrase "lol", which can be used to indicate that the problem might not be that serious or that they are just so obsessed with texting acronyms that it is impossible for them to stop, could also be an indication that the person is just too enthralled by the idea of laughing. It is still a major offense to flirtexting.

If flirtexting is being used to propel your relationship to a higher level, and you want it become real, then don't try to diminish it with cutesy acronyms and text talk.

That text message should be saved for messages with friends or exasperated family members. But not for the one that you are truly into. You shouldn't expect to be treated like a seven year-old by texting.

LOL, OMG and other acronyms can be confusing. Although everyone may know what these acronyms are, your crush will likely be confused by them.

There is nothing that can halt a conversation quicker than someone texting back "???. Not the response you were looking for?

Imagine you've just texted your sweetheart a "TOY" message and they reply "???. Now you must explain that TOY refers to "thinking of" your sweetheart. It would have been quicker, simpler and much more meaningful to just send thinking about me in the first place.

There's no need to flirt too often or too little.

People wonder if texting is excessive or not enough without actually talking about it. These are not rules but there might be some guidelines that can help you, especially when you're just starting out in a new relationship.

The general rules of texting are:

Never send out text messages that are not answered.

Sending back to back messages demanding responses is not a good idea. You might not like the response you get.

If your guy is overstressed, busy, or involved in school or work, don't text him.

Flirtexting has a few extra rules, such as:

If your flirty texts don't get the desired response, then you might consider resending them.

If you find your messages becoming repetitive and boring, or if the responses seem too short and clipped than usual, it could be an indication that you are overdoing things.

You should not send a flirty or distracting text to someone who is already very busy with something or a project.

Don't be caught in the Octopus of Love

There are many fascinating things about the modern world. One is the ability of friends and family to communicate in many ways, sometimes simultaneously. You can also text.

You can message them on Instagram, Twitter or Facebook. Although you can do these things, you should not try to do them all at once.

Stop texting people and simultaneously sending them messages through any other platform.

Stop waiting two seconds to send the same message or a similar one to another platform. It makes you seem clingy. It makes you look desperate.

It is quite obvious that it makes you look crazy. Choose a venue to send your message, then wait for a return.

Chapter 17: How to Respect It With Class and Sass

Exchanging contact information is the first step to text messaging. Then, either party can initiate a conversation. The process of familiarity can take some time. It starts with learning how your potential spouse communicates, likes and dislikes, along with the preferred method of text messaging. Extra effort is required to keep your relationship strong through text messaging. It is important to not let your desperation show in your communications and messaging.

Men will become bored easily if they feel that they are the center of your lives, even before you get to know them well. This is because men are wired to chase after women. Turning that around can cause contempt. It is not easy to maintain class and sassy, especially when emotions are involved. If one party reacts too strongly, it can lead to disrespect for the other.

Texting Attitudes

To maintain a respectful conversation, text messaging shouldn't be misused. You should evaluate how texting is integrated into your life and how dependent you are on it. The rule is more similar to what individuals often recommend. First, work on yourself before dealing with others. When texting is used to socialize, you don't want any bad attitude towards texting that could make your potential spouse or another person in your relationship uncomfortable. Worries about your significant other not listening could cause unhealthy communication and relationships. Recognizing limitations to communication via texting is the start of self-monitoring.

Texting attitudes are influenced by your childhood communication style, as well as how you interact with other people in the new environment. These attitudes can prevent seamless communication and expose you to being emotionally unclassy and immature.

Self-disclosure attitudes

This is a form of communication in which one person shares information about themselves to another. This type of expression includes feelings, hopes and dreams. The anxiety that comes along with the idea of self-disclosure and the freedom to express yourself freely is called the attitude of self disclosure. In most cases it leads to withdrawal from speaking with and interaction with another person. If the other person is more open and comfortable, it could make you seem stifling and insecure.

Miscommunication and attitude

Texting can lead to miscommunication. Communication could become a problem if you adopt this attitude when you receive or send a text. This will affect the way you feel about each other texting. This will often lead to a judgemental attitude and block genuine communication.

The Attitude of Social Connectivity

These people believe that being able initiate and keep an online conversation is a great way to connect with others. However, this attitude can be detrimental to texting. You will believe your social connections will be affected if you don't have an online life, like texting. This kind of attitude could lead you to be depressed and start texting constantly as though it is your life or death. The other party could end up stepping out of their digital space. This can make it difficult for them to get back on track. The right amount of text messaging should not be used to disrupt the social connection. It allows both parties to have fun and gives them the opportunity to practice respectful texting with others.

Attitude of concern

This is the fear of texting. It could be due to past experiences. A conversation that is fraught with anxiety can lead to a misunderstanding and turn off potential partners. You may avoid having a conversation via text message because you might end up using too many plugins, such as emoji, and send one-word replies. This could make it difficult to express your brilliance. Your apprehension could stem from an unfortunate event or someone who was affected by online communication. While it may not be common, this is a serious problem and can hinder the discussion.

Attitude of Expectancy

Once the intention is established and communication on various topics has begun, it is essential that you remain cool and not expect too many things. Expectancy leads to fear of rejection. If you get upset about not being met, or get too emotional on the phone, it could lead you to blame the recipient for the slow response culture. In the real sense of the word, the individual is held high by their activity. This kind of attitude will cause you to lose respect for your partner and can lead to arguments and even a rift. This is another error made by someone who has unrealistic expectations. It could happen that you are in your office in the middle-of-the-morning, just after a long meeting, and decide on chatting with your partner about last night. Unfortunately, it goes unanswered for many hours. In real life, your partner was giving a presentation for his bosses that lasted two hours and had spent considerable time preparing. Because you expect high standards from the other person, it can make your partner feel discourteous.

Texting Etiquette With Class and Sass

Self-monitoring helps you to keep a respectful and professional relationship with texting, despite all the possible mistakes. For couples that have been together for years, it is crucial to learn how to text properly. No matter whether your spouse is your partner, maintaining digital respect automatically contributes towards a healthy and happy relationship.

This is your goal: to keep a man close by you once you have bagged him. By being a good man, you can demonstrate your self-worth and intelligence. Sassiness can be described as a personality trait that is mostly associated with old age. This means you are able to convey your message with honesty and bluntness in a different style than being pushy, arrogant, or pushy. It takes the right wit and ability to discern when it is appropriate to add a bit of sassiness to a conversation without offending your spouse. It can be quite difficult to identify a sassy woman's temperament from one who isn't. This is because they have the ability to manage their emotional distress and will always find ways to remain calm.

Reply to a Message with a Message

A text message can be very exciting, especially if it is a personal message. It is tempting to just reply to a simple text, such as "hey how are you today?" and then call the recipient to ask questions. This can be rude and unprofessional. The other party expects mutual communication, taking into account their day's work schedule and activities. This can come across as desperate or impatience. Either you are too busy and don't have the time or are too inactive, so you prefer to have a call rather than messages. Both of these actions will be perceived as inconsiderate by the other party, and could lead to them staying away. These actions are unacceptable for a woman who is a classy lady and brings sass to a party.

Use Witty Comebacks & Sarcasm

Sometimes your potential partner might be reluctant about texting. While it's possible to call someone out for their bad behavior in class and sass, you should avoid assertiveness or rudeness. Even though sassy or class can sometimes be blocked by emotions and feelings, it works well for you if you are able to string the right words together in an adult way to convey your point. Instead of using intimidation tactics to elicit hurtful remarks, this shows maturity.

The Daily Schedule is worth looking at

Even though a relationship can appear to be a full-time job or task, everyone has a daily schedule. It could be either at work, school running errands and even traveling for business. Sometimes, it is possible to be disrespectful and overstep when you bag the man. If you are an early bird, you might get on the road to work by 5:05 AM. But the other person may be working late and put off getting up. This is why it might not be a good idea to send multiple text messages at the same time. It can be very distracting to receive a barrage text message that begins with 'good morning', a single conversation between the messages, and a last 'good afternoon' text. It's exhausting and might cause other parties to ignore you.

Pay attention to the language

Lady with class and sass needs language that is accurate and correct. To avoid sending gibberish or confusing messages, it is important to double-check text autocorrect. This will result in the conversation becoming less focused and less important. Since your way of encoding languages is different, it is essential to pay close attention to symbols, abbreviations, and emoji. You may not want to use the same street language as you are used to. It can be offensive to use the wrong abbreviation like "LOL" when you are texting your partner. This could mean that you have 'lots' of love. Text messages without this attention are indicative of a careless person who lacks communication skills.

Keep Your Texts Positive

You might be tempted to share everything with your partner, even if you are on a journey of getting to know each other better. You should be careful not to go too public. It's common for people to confide in their partners when they are in the company or with total strangers. This could lead to a negative culture and a loss of attraction for your partner. Not texting your boss about how traffic has made your day miserable and your boss is uncaring is a bad idea. Most people are going through similar difficulties. It is difficult to ignore obvious obstacles, which no one wants or needs to hear. Intelligence and maturity can help you get past them. You don't have to pretend you're insincere or are fakeing the relationship. However, being cheerful and lively will make your partner want more conversations.

Stop overcrowding his space

Digital space is important. You should be careful about text messaging and only send it when you are absolutely necessary. It can quickly become monotonous to text and send unnecessary messages, which could make your partner feel uncomfortable. This mysteriousness is what keeps the spark alive. The time spent between texts can also make your partner miss you. Allowing your partner to have space can help prepare you for a great dinner date or casual hangout. It is important to maintain a professional appearance so you have good memories.

Keep It Sexy, But Not Ratchet

The conversation can lead to couples sexting. This is not everyone's cup of tea. You should take it slowly and keep your classy and sass intact. The transmission of sexual content should be an intellectual process, not overwhelming and overbearing. For example, some people may find posting pornographic photos or videos while texting annoying. However, others might find this acceptable. Do your homework about texting. Find out what your partner prefers. You can also take a chance and show your partner some basic sexting skills. Ratchetness can be associated with uncouthness, mannerlessness, and is a detriment to the gender. Sexting can be misinterpreted by the recipient, and they may have strange or unorthodox ideas. Your intention could simply be to keep things interesting without actually engaging in sexual activity.

Between the Lines

It is different to how you communicate with people via text message from others. Individuals are different in their ability to express themselves. This is why it is crucial that you take the time to read a simple message from your partner. Sometimes your partner might be tired at work or on the road taking care of an emergency. But they can't explain this to you via text. You can see signs they might be distracted or not feeling the need to talk on text in one sentence. If you push for discussion, you may end up being annoyed at your partner or drowning in unnecessary assumptions. The ability to use your intelligence and discern whether it is the right time for you to engage in text messaging with someone shows maturity.

Keep It Clear and Precise

If you have a lot of information to communicate, it is likely that you will text paragraph after paragraph to your mother or a colleague, spouse, friend, or spouse. If you do this, your spouse will not tolerate it. Men dislike long messages and details that are difficult to understand. Even when you are feeling resentful, it is best that you keep long conversations short and save them for a one-on-1 meeting or phone conversation. You can send long text messages and it is too overwhelming. It could make the recipient feel like a nagger and a clinger. The recipient may find it hard to take in the long-windedness and the excitement that comes with it.

Chapter 18: Influencing Someone Through Text

Here things get interesting. We have become so dependent on texting to communicate with people, it has caused us a slight handicap in terms of influencing others. You don't have the option of using body language or other methods of persuasion. You can influence someone to agree to your idea simply by nodding your heads while stating it. To give someone comfort and trust, touch them on the shoulder as you make a statement. These actions are impossible to perform with texting.

There are many ways you can influence someone regardless of whether they are communicating via text or face-to-face.

Let's take a look at ten different ways you can influence someone.

1. The Benjamin Franklin effect

Legend has it that Benjamin Franklin once asked a man who didn't know him if he could borrow his rare book. Franklin, who had never met Franklin before, graciously thanked Franklin for his book. Scientists confirmed this theory when they found out that those who were asked by the researcher for personal favors rated the researcher higher than the others. Although it may sound odd, when someone does a favor on you, it is likely that their brain will conclude that you are worthy of the favor. It is important that they like you. This can be done by asking for advice. It is important to validate the advice you get by asking someone for their opinion and not others.

2. Flattery is your ticket to success:

Flattery is one way to get what your heart desires, but it must be sincere. There is a high chance that flattery will backfire. Cognitive balance is something that most people aim for. It's important to organize thoughts and feelings in the same way. If you flatter someone with high self confidence, you are validating their views about themselves. However, flattery can do more harm to someone with low self confidence than good. This is because it affects their perception of themselves.

3. Get your tongue in there:

What does it make you feel when someone tells your wrong opinion about something? Does it make you more comfortable with the person? Most likely not. You don't have to tell them that you are wrong. There are ways to communicate your disagreement and make it pleasant. Instead of making a point of their error, you can listen to them and explain what your position is. They will be more inclined to hear what you have to share and will let you correct them without you realizing. It is important to admit when you make mistakes. It will make it easier for you to be trusted and considerate.

4. You can't call a rose a rose under any other name.

Anyone who has read a basic psychology text will tell them that repeating a person's name is their favorite sound. A person's name is an important part of their identity. Hearing someone else's name can help them feel more confident and happy about themselves. This can be used to transform someone into what you want. By calling your employer "boss", you can validate their position by boosting their ego. If you repeatedly refer to someone's name as "boss", it will have the same effect if they are used their name again and again.

Because it is less subtle than in normal conversation, you need to exercise caution when using this technique in texting.

5. Mirror, mirror at the wall

We are all vane creatures. We love our own self more than we love the other. This is why we are open and positive to those who imitate our movements and gestures. This psychology also applies to texting. The mirror effect will cause you to feel more connected by mimicking another's writing style or using emoticons and words.

6. In other words:

One powerful way to influence someone is by showing them empathy. This can be done by paraphrasing their words and repeating them to them. This is called reflective listening. It allows people to communicate more emotions to each other. This can be especially effective when done via texting. The person can then read what they have texted and rephrase it in a question to confirm that you get them. They will be more inclined to listen to what they have to say if you show you care.

7. The right place, at the right moment:

Tired or mentally tired people are much more open-minded and willing to submit. To influence someone to do something they may not agree to, wait to send a text message. This could be in their last hour at work, or late at night. They will probably respond with "I'll do it tomorrow" and, since humans usually keep their word, it is likely that they will follow up on their promise.

8. Yes, Drill Sergeant :

Everyone doesn't like feeling compelled to do certain things. People will respond more favorably when you ask them to do something than if they tell you. This method is powerful because emoticons can be used to convey your feelings. A friendly smiley and a cheeky smile can make someone feel even more convincing.

9. The Don Corleone

The Godfather is an example of how to make a person accept an offer. Begin with a small favor instead of asking for large amounts. If someone has already pledged to something smaller, it will make it easier to ask them for a larger favor later. It is natural for us to agree to second requests after we have accepted the first. Psychologically speaking though, it's better for you to wait a few more days before asking for the second request.

10. A picture can paint a thousand sentences:

Visually impaired people, particularly men, are more likely to agree with something than others. If there is visual stimulation, we are more likely than not to agree with it. Texting offers the obvious advantage of being capable of using any type of image, video, chart, or graph to influence others. If information is provided by a third party, it's a plus. People are inclined to follow the herd. If you can show that people have already accepted what you propose, it will make it easier to convince them.

Electronic Seduction: What is the Art?

No matter how much you think that you know about seduction you are still learning. You may have wondered what seduction means when it is called "art". You can always improve your skills, just as with playing a musical instrument and painting on canvas. Your art will improve as you practice more. The same applies to seduction. It's even more important in this modern age where certain social constructs are changing more frequently than before. The use of texting and email to seduce people has become very popular, and is the preferred method for "breaking the ice".

This is, in part, because of the relative ease with which texting can be used. It's much easier to have your message rejected privately than it is in person. However, it is much easier for the person refusing to accept the rejection to be honest. They don't feel as obligated to spare the feelings and opinions of the other person.

While seduction is a part and parcel of human interaction, both men & women are affected by it. But the approaches to each gender are very different. Nevertheless, there are some things that remain constant.

Women and men would not want to look desperate or needy, for example. Necessity is not the most attractive trait one can have, and it may make the other person feel pressured. It is important to avoid being needy. Nonchalant behavior will demonstrate to the other that you accept yourself and see yourself as independent. Avoid appearing arrogant by not being too assertive.

How can you make it easy for someone to text you?

Face-to–face interaction can help you communicate the attitude that devil-may-care.

However, texting is not a bad idea. Here are some rules that apply to both men and ladies.

Avoid bombarding the other person in messages. It gives off the impression that your life is boring and you have nothing to do. This means that you should not text chat. You should only send short but valuable messages. They should be intelligent, mature and stimulating. (SMS).

Timing is everything. It doesn't matter if they don't reply within 24 hours, or for a few days. You don't care if they reply (as long as they are concerned). The modern texting app will let you know when they read your message. If they don't reply immediately, this could indicate that they are busy or are not interested in you. They don't want to appear too eager. Don't reply to text messages immediately.

Be careful what kind of humor you use. It is not possible to truly understand the humor of a person you don't know. Offending someone is the last thing you want when trying to seduce.

Use correct grammar. While not everyone can be Ernest Hemmingway (although autocorrect is available on most smartphones), there's no reason to make yourself look ignorant or lazy. Bad grammar in text is equivalent to being lazy in real life.

Try to keep the other person's attention by remaining mysterious. If you're being asked about your day or the weekend, you can be mysterious and keep the other person interested. You should be careful not to respond with text messages that are too brief. Don't reply "good, mine?" to questions about how your day was. You don't want your answers to seem disinterested. It can be very difficult to find the right balance, especially since tone and body language are missing.

The most important rule: Be seductive, and not deceptive. When you only want a relationship and not a long-term one, seducing someone will lead to a negative reputation. Look at the person you are interested in to see if they are searching for the same things that you are. It is important to be honest with your partner if you want to start a relationship. It will eliminate anyone who only wants a physical encounter.

Chapter 19: Tips for keeping things spicy with sexting

Let's face it, a long relationship can get boring and even repetitive. It is hard to love your partner but you long for things to be as exciting and fun as they were at the beginning. Technology offers solutions. You don't want your lover to hear, "Hey my love, you bores me in bed". It's understandable. Nobody wants to hear that they have boring sex. You can ignite the spark with some sexting. Send some tantalizing sexts to get out of your pajamas. Wear something sensual instead.

Here is a list with the most popular sexting messages. Choose from the following messages, customize them and be mindful that some messages may be gender-specific. This is also a good idea to ensure that the recipient is the right person.

What are you wearing?

You want to play a sport? Are you the only one?

I was thinking of you while I was showering.

I have a super sexy surprise in store for you.

I am wearing all red, even my underwear.

What would you prefer me to wear for the next time?

Let's get to know each other.

Do you see the car from the back tonight?

It's not my heart that throbs when you're near me.

Your lips are sensuous. Let me kiss the ones that I can't.

If you are feeling tired, I will offer a massage.

Do you want scream tonight?

I also like to play with your hair, and other things.

You know what buttons to push.

If I ever see you, I will show you the love that I have for you.

I don't need porn. All I need is your sexy body.

Why do you make me hungry?

Wear something that will keep me guessing next time I meet you.

I will take you on an amazing vacation to orgasm.

Would you like to see my 50th shade of grey?

I am restless. Will you come by and tie my hands?

I want you to give me permission to be rough.

Tonight I'll be your prisoner.

I would love to share my life with you.

If you could read my mind, I would blush right here.

You can make me feel so miserable just by looking at my face.

Meet me later? I want to have something delicious.

I'm going tap it when you pass by me next.

Are you looking to update your wardrobe?

Let me be the best fantasy.

I saw you mostly naked in your dream last night.

You can almost make me orgasm by just looking at me.

I want peaches with cream tonight. Are you free to do other things?

I want to drizzle chocolate syrup over your body, and then clean my teeth.

Are you all alone tonight? I don't want anyone hearing you scream.

I have a surprise waiting for you. It is in my pants.

It makes me happy just to look at your pictures.

Just the thought of touching your skin gives me goose bumps.

I want all night to go.

Is your prey?

Whip cream is my favorite dessert. Would you allow me to spread it on you

I have a strategy for us. It involves my bed.

Just to let everyone know that I really like riding with you.

I am interested in learning some sexy moves. Do you have any suggestions?

I'm so horny, and you are so far away.

I have a move that I want to show you.

If you like it, you shouldn't resist it.

You make me squeamish; I'm done.

I like your tie.

Don't waste your energy on me, I have something you can do.

Frisk me; deep.

I'd love to see yours if it was mine.

Use this list as a guideline for sexting with your partner. Let's discuss when is the best time to sext your partner. A sext is considered hot and teasing if it occurs in an unresponsive situation, such as at work or at a social event. It can turn into a hot, dirty little secret. This is what most men find to be annoying. However, this is also true for women.

If you discover that you and your significant other have separated for any reason you should stop talking to each other. You can sext to ignite that "newfound relationship" spark you once had. It's a great way to get dirty and sexy. You should start the hot conversation with a flirtatious tone, before you move on to more sensitive messages.

It's a good idea to use sexting as a way to get sexy foreplay. If you and your significant others are present with other people but still sitting together or in the exact same room, send them a steamy, steamy text. You can see their facial expressions while they read the text. Next, you can send another text commenting about how they responded. It will make your partner happy and get them ready for when they return. It is important to follow up.

Chapter 20: How You Build and Maintain Attraction

They believe that Mars is home to men, Venus is home to women. This doesn't necessarily mean that women and men can not have something in common. Actually, opposites attract (pardon for the cliches).

How can you keep the man interested in every word you speak? It's all in the girl. It is important to think like you would to attract a woman. It doesn't matter if you act like a man. However, it is important that you let your man know that you could be his male friend.

You don't necessarily have to claim that you are an expert on everything.

Men find it annoying when you try to pretend that you know everything. You can hook your guy by doing some research.

What topics draw men to you?

1. Sports - it's very obvious that even nerdy guys can have a league of there own

2. Women

3. Sex

But this does not mean you must limit yourself to what is mentioned. It is okay to not be comfortable with any three topics. Sometimes it is simply a matter to learn how to talk and text men to win their undying love. Here are some tips to help you talk and text men in order to keep them attracted.

It is important to get to know you first. By knowing yourself, you will be able sell your self to anyone. Know both your strengths and weaknesses. You don't have to think extravagantly about yourself. Think about what makes you stand out from the rest. Because that's what makes you different, it is what makes your personality unique. This is what will make you a magnet for your man.

Men don't like it when women talk too much. Second, remember to pay attention to the headlines when talking or texting. Keep it brief. Keep it short. You want them to ask for more and not get bored. You will have awkward silences, but there is nothing wrong in a conversation that pauses.

Relax, keep calm, and get rid of any unneeded thoughts.

You can take control of the discussion and change the direction if it becomes too boring or negative. It is not common for men to be able to leave a topic that they don't feel comfortable with, even though they may not want to admit it. Perhaps they are just being gentlemanly. They can actually shut down when it gets difficult and just zone out. This does not have to be the case. This is because women do it better than you, the boss. No questions asked.

One word of warning: Men hate women who are desperate. They don't love to see your life and how your happiness is dependent on them. Take it one spoon at time. Women have a tendency to plan six months in advance. Men hate this. Keep calm and composed.

This is how men should be treated. Before we get into the details of the techniques, which can be both basic and advanced, it's important that you are familiar with the basics of texting. Next chapter will be about texting rules.

Chapter 21: What Not to Text

Here are some things you should never text to men if you want their attention.

Mundane detail:

You're not texting with your BFF. You can't expect him to be interested at all times of your life. You will frustrate him and he will quickly get bored. He doesn't seem to care that you are buying sandals that perfectly match the dress you purchased last week. Are you able to take him shopping at the mall? No? He would not enjoy text messaging a play-by play of the same play.

Boring Texts

Although I do not believe every text should be filled full of intrigue and excitement, it is important to remember that they are all different. When you write "I'm bored", what are you actually saying? It's possible to think that you want to tell him I'm tired of doing nothing and that I'm boring. But if he would just come over and ask me out, then I would find life exciting!" This is not what he's hearing.

He thinks "Hmmm." when you send him a text saying "I'm really bored". If she can't think up anything to entertain herself, she must have been boring. Do you think she has any friends? If I choose to date her, she will always expect me be the one to plan where and how we should go. I don't want a partner who I have to entertain.

Okay. He may not believe all of it. It's the impression you give. This is because you expect others to keep you entertained. If they don't, then you're bored.

And, what do you mean by "I'm bored"? "Sorry, that's so disappointing."

Another boring text to read is "What you doing?" and the ever-popular "hey". You can do better than that. You can do better.

Here are some alternatives:

"I heard something fascinating about you" You don't think any guy will want to know what it was. This is why you will need some evidence. But, don't tell the guy right away. Keep him guessing.

Numerous Grammar and Spelling Errors

You can take a few minutes to review your text before you respond. You're unlikely to be dropped by him for a typo. If every message you send contains mistakes, he'll get a very clear picture of your intelligence. It is possible you've been told by some that dumb chicks are a favorite of guys. You may have heard that dumb men love dumb chicks. To keep a relationship with a texting partner going, you need to be challenged and excited.

Wrong Numbers - Texts

This is embarrassing. You want to send a text about Mike to your friend, but you already know his name so you text him. Awkward! It is best to double-check all your texts before hitting send. You can save yourself a lot by taking the time to double-check your text before you hit send.

Accusations & Jealous Rants

"I've been texting you all day ???? What were your last names? ?"

"I saw Julie and I at the movies yesterday. Does this mean that you are interested in her rather than me?

He will most likely think that he is a "PSYCHO ALERT!" and you won't hear back from him again. If you're in a relationship with someone and suspect he's cheating, it is best to confront him in person. However, if he hasn't asked you out yet, then it is time to calm down. You don't have control over him.

Ultimatums

"Are you interested or not in me? You don't have to be interested, just let me know. I have plenty of guys waiting to meet you. This is the last message I will send you."

You can see why this doesn't work. It can make you look needy, and even a little crazy. It will not spark jealousy.

If he does not text you first and stops replying to your messages, and if he never asks you out, it's a sign that he isn't interested. Not right now. Perhaps things will change in time.

Unless he thinks you are needy and crazy.

You can find someone to help you now. I didn't mean to say, "use someone other than him to make them jealous." Talk to guys to find someone you actually want to spend time.

Explicit Photos

I will be completely honest and say that this is never a good idea. Do not send photos via phone unless it is your intention for the photo to be posted on the internet. I get it. You think he would never do such a thing. It's possible that he might. Particularly if you can find someone nicer or cuter than him and then dump him. Perhaps he's a jerk. And lastly, even though he may not have done so, it is possible that he has friends who are able to access his phone occasionally and don't care much about your feelings. He could even lose his phone by accident or have it stolen.

Plus, explicit photos will not make him less interested in you. It sounds like it could. But it doesn't. It eliminates the tension, attraction, and self-confidence you worked so hard for.

Sexting

It works in the same way as the photos. Making a few sexual comments and flirting with a guy can be very attractive. Exaggerated texts and graphic details can take the mystery out. Playful innuendo attracts. Sexting is an excellent way to be humiliated before a lot people.

It's not difficult for one his friends to take his phone. Remember what I said above about the photos. You don't have to send the conversation unless you're willing for it to be published on Facebook pages or shared on YouTube. Send it and it will disappear.

Drinking and texting

This is a dangerous combination. You might regret saying things and, worse, you won't be able to remember them.

Chapter 22: Building Comfort

Implied disqualifiers

The mistake that guys make is asking too much of their girl and trying to make too many plans at once. This can make the girl feel uncomfortable and she will stop responding. If you want to make her feel at ease, it is a good idea to tell her you are unable to make plans. After that, continue texting as normal.

It is important to say that you are not interested in meeting up soon with her because you are too busy or you are out of town. This lets her know that although you do not intend to ask you out on a date or set an agenda for the future, you still care about getting to know you. This will make her respond more positively to you than if she expects something from you.

She will feel less awkward about you having to turn down and will enjoy your interactions more. You could say it to her and tell them that you'd like to get better acquainted before meeting up.

Connection and digging deeper into your questions

The girl may not feel that she is able to trust you if you just send them funny memes or flirty messages. It might be worth your time to make a connection via text to show her that you care about her.

Girls love to express their feelings more than men. When she asks you how you are, you can respond in two ways. You can tell your friend you are feeling good, then stop and question her. You can also describe a feeling that you experienced that day and tell her what led you to feel that way. This will let girls know that you are more than just the surface.

You need to ask the right questions. If she tells us she is working on painting, we can ask where she got her inspiration. We can also ask her how it feels to finish a painting. You will be able to learn more about her by asking questions.

When you meet up with her in the next step, it is important to have a general idea of the girl's comfort level. If she doesn't feel adventurous, you may not want her to meet up late or go somewhere new. This could mean that you will need to be more familiar with her area in order to feel comfortable enough to say yes.

Why you should contact her

You can test your comfort level by asking her to speak with you on the phone. If a girl loves you enough, she will answer your phone. Some girls are not comfortable speaking on the telephone, but if they feel you have the right frame of mind with you, they will pick up your phone.

If they don't respond, it might mean they aren't yet comfortable enough with you. This could indicate that they have not found the right person for them and may need to take additional steps to make them feel valued and attract you. As a general rule, girls feel less pressure to lead the conversation than guys, and are therefore less anxious to speak on the phone.

You can build trust with a girl by talking on the telephone with her. It is common for guys to forget that the phone can also be used to make calls. Communication via text is more powerful than calling and talking to someone. It is much easier to get the girl to call you than it is to text.

The mid-text calling

If you find yourself engaged in a full-blown text conversation with the girl where both of your messages are lengthy, you can rest assured that she will return her call if she's halfway through.

You can use this excuse if you are texting back and forth: "I don't know what to think about you, but I am tired of looking at screens all day. Would you like to have a conversation? ".

Unless she's in a place that she cannot talk, you can be certain that she'll say yes. Talking to her over the phone will make it much easier for her.

What if she isn't available to answer the phone?

If you have a history with calling, you can simply send it as a missed message and leave no messages.

If this is your first time calling her, and she doesn't pick up, you could just say "hey, guess that you're busy" and then simply text what you meant to say. Don't make a big deal.

Even if she doesn't answer, that doesn't mean you need to stop asking questions. It's important to respond the same way that you would with your friend.

Conclusion

Most of these techniques work for men of any type, but they can be customized to suit the needs of each man.

Once you build confidence, you can start to text men more frequently and get their attention faster. If you are unsure if you should do a trial run before messaging the boy of your dreams then ask a friend for help. He can text you to test your flirting.

You can ask him for corrections if you make mistakes and tell him where you are succeeding. Once you believe you have what it takes, you can start messaging the dream boy and convince him to love you.

www.ingramcontent.com/pod-product-compliance
Lightning Source LLC
Chambersburg PA
CBHW050025130526
44590CB00042B/1910